Extreme Couponing

Without

Extreme Stress

Sara Hailey &
Brenda Trott

First Printing, 2012

Printed in the United States of America

**ISBN-13:
978-1463684457**

**ISBN-10:
1463684452**

Liability Disclaimer

By reading this document, you assume all risks associated with using the advice given below, with a full understanding that you, solely, are responsible for anything that may occur as a result of putting this information into action in any way and regardless of your interpretation of the advice.

Be warned: once you start saving, it is hard to stop!

Contents

1. Who this book is for

Everyone loves a deal. Perhaps you're old enough to remember banks offering free toasters for opening an account. How about the sad day S&H Green Stamps closed their doors no longer providing free merchandise to their loyal customers?

This book is for those who want to make use of today's deals: coupons, sales, special promotions, and rebates. People who can make good use of this book include:

- People like Sara, contemplating a second job
- People who have made a commitment to climb out of debt
- Stay at home moms or dads who want to make a contribution to the household budget
- People looking for extra money to start a college fund, invest in a 401k, start a business, buy something special or (you fill in the blank)
- Someone who thinks they don't have the time or energy to coupon

Who is Sara

Sara Hailey is the founder of epiccouponing.com, the Director of her church youth group, Organizer of the Church Impact Group (for adults between youth and retirement) and the facilitator of couponing workshops. Her real job remains a wife of 14 years and the mother of four very active children. Her children play sports and have regular activities that keep her family on the move at a constant pace. So time is precious. She must make the most of her spare time and use it wisely.

Sara soon found herself studying the Extreme Coupon show on TLC and said to herself "I can do that!" Six weeks later she began her first extreme shopping trip and she hasn't gone back. Sara has told many people she doesn't care if she wins the lottery, "I will never pay retail again". She started saving so much in such a short time that her husband was amazed. Prior to coupons, it was a common occurrence for her family to spend in excess of $800 on groceries every month. With a teenager and a few pre-teens in the house, food disappeared fast! She has been able to get her grocery bill down to around $200 a month. That is a huge jump from $800. Couponing has become a very important source of income for Sara and her family. Couponing is also a family affair. The kids learned to cut, sort, and shop too.

Sara even got her church youth group involved in her coupon obsession. Since the church is such a big part of her family life, she has found a way to incorporate them as well. When she coupons, she is always on the look out for snacks and drinks for the youth group. Once, she was able to donate 25- 2 liter soda bottles and many times she has donated various snacks. She even has them collecting expired coupons to send to the troops. The youth group kids are always excited to help out the troops. The entire church collects and brings their coupons to the youth group and they in turn package them up and send them to the soldiers.

Who is Brenda

Brenda, a mother of four, is raising an army of bargain hunters. Although she and her family are always on the look out for ways to save money, her time is limited because she runs two businesses and writes for several venues.

Brenda is an educator, an author, and an entre-preneur. Her resume includes growing a home business into several different locations and eventually landing a contract with a local university. She has profited from running trade shows which raise funds for non-profit organizations and taught nearly every level of school. Her passion, remains writing informative articles and ebooks and ghost writing biographies.

Although addicted to bargains, Brenda despises shopping. She can think of a thousand different things to do with her time than to spend it at a store. She depends on organization and kid power to get her grocery shopping done.

The world of coupons has opened up another side of life for Brenda and she feels as though she belongs to a wonderful new club of people living a frugal lifestyle. She doesn't make couponing a part-time job but she does enjoy the extra savings for her family.

Why we wrote this book

Brenda and Sara's first encounter was at the Chamber of Commerce meeting in the small town of Tomball, TX. In a crowd of over 300 stuffy lawyers, insurance, and real estate agents, Sara stood on stage with a goofy looking hat. She revived the audience with her quirky energy and let everyone in the room know about her up-coming fundraiser. She was charging the tiny sum of $5 to attend her class on Extreme Couponing. All of the proceeds went to support the youth group at her church.

Brenda saw a story in Sara and wrote a promotional piece plugging the class. She later brought a friend along to the class but was skeptical. How much could she learn about clipping coupons? She was absolutely amazed at what she learned and couldn't wait to put it into action.

While Brenda toyed around with the idea of writing an ebook, she wasn't sure how to approach Sara. Great minds really do think alike, because Sara ended up contacting her and wanted some help writing a guide. Between the two of us you get the mistakes and triumphs of a novice and an expert. Lucky you!

How we clip the stress out of couponing

This book is designed as a step by step guide to help you get the most out of your coupons without adding a bunch of stress to your life. We tell you what mistakes to avoid and how to keep yourself motivated to save. We offer time saving tips and tricks to get you from the clipping through the checkout with ease. From just buying what is on sale, all the way to stockpiling and getting "paid" to shop.

Sara's wall of fame

Showcased below are just a few of Sara's triumphs. After about 6 months of extreme shopping, Sara took an inventory and added up the value of her pantry. Taking care to list only items she used coupons to purchase, she found the retail value of these items was $981.84 but her cost after coupons was only $129.61, that's a savings of $852.23!!!

What could you do with an extra $800 or so?

Sara wasn't done there. Next she took an inventtory of the items in her upper level stockpile. This is where she stored all the toiletry and paper goods. The retail value of these items was $2259.88 but her cost after coupons was $158.82! That's $2101.06 in savings!!!! It doesn't take a rocket scientist to know that adds up to HUGE savings!

Would an extra $2,000 or so put a dent in your monthly mortgage?

Here is yet another example of savings in Sara's own words:

> For my birthday, my dear sweet husband wanted to get me something that I have wanted for a very very long time. He actually went to the mall, which is a place be hates to go, and bought me my first Coach purse. He picked it out himself and it was really really pretty. He did good! He was telling me that they had all different styles and shapes and sizes, and told me that if I wanted I could take it back and pick out the one I wanted. I loved the one he got me, but when I looked at the receipt, I couldn't believe that he had paid retail for the purse. He paid over $500!
>
> Needless to say I was shocked: happy, but shocked. I took the purse and the receipt to the outlet mall instead. I love the outlet mall, because they have good deals all the time! When I walked in, they were handing out 30% off coupons, which is awesome! For the same price that he paid for one purse at the regular mall, I got two purses, a wallet and a key-chain! I was so stoked! I came home and showed him my results! He was excited too. I loved that it also gave me an opportunity to go shopping. This would have been a great story but there is more. Later that same week, I went to check the mail and surprise! Coach had sent my husband a $50 gift certificate as a thank you for

shopping with them at the mall. YAY!; another reason to go shopping. So, I went and then got another wallet, completely FREE! Using coupons extends past the grocery store. Coupons are available for everything now!

From purses to outings with the family, to hair cuts, to amusement parks; you can find coupons for absolutely everything. Never pay retail again!

Brenda's first month

Brenda started off slow. She purchased two papers (for $2.00 each) on Sunday. She cut out all of the coupons in the car while her family drove to a store in town. The papers were paid for the moment they used a buy one get one free restaurant coupon at a place they had already decided to eat. She was excited that she hadn't wasted her money yet. By Friday she had saved over $30 buying only things she normally bought.

Brenda opted to buy 3 papers the next week and after 10 total shopping minutes she saved $56 and had scored free toothbrushes and shampoo. This was the week she wished she had bought more newspapers!

Brenda's excitement started to wane on her friends but that didn't stop her from following one around Walmart during her 3rd week. Her friend shopped as usual and didn't even notice

Brenda pulling out coupons along the way. At the register she handed the cashier $6.00 in coupons and price matched 5 other items. Her friend saved nearly $20 without planning but she had to buy Brenda dinner!

Overview

Step by step, this book will show you the value in using coupons and teach you how to over come your own objections to saving money. Once you have made the commitment to give this couponing thing a try, we'll guide you through the acquisition of coupons, organization of supplies, and developing a system for shopping that works for you. Everyone is different, so finding the organizational style that works for you is key to your success in couponing.

This book will give you the organizational skills and ideas that will keep you successful and revved up about couponing. Several of our steps will show you how to get by with the minimum, and some will show you how to push a little further or go extreme and really get the most out of your time.

We will show you how to stay motivated, budget your time, and choose a simple system to find your deals. We will give you the short cuts and time saving tips we learned through trial and error and we will remind you to have fun!

Warning! This is Addictive!

Even if you're not sure you can fit this couponing thing into your life, once you get started saving all that money, you will be hooked. Go ahead and start off slow, but realize that saving money is very addictive! Once you get that very first "free" item, you won't want to wait to go home and find more deals! You might get so good at this that others will call you "that crazy coupon person." Just note, that we told you so!

2. Is it Worth It?

Each dip in the economy and trace of a recession offers the local newspapers a great marketing tool: coupons! Most newspapers list the dollar value of all the included coupons right on the front page as an enticement to get you to buy the paper. With everyone across the nation buckling down and tightening their budgets, companies are relying more than ever on coupons for their advertising.

Even with the recent explosion of excited coupon clippers proclaiming their savings on a daily basis on blogs, websites, TV, and radio many people still have stumbling blocks that keep them from saving some serious cash. How many of these excuses have you used?

Common Excuses:

"I wish I had the time"
Extreme couponing can take a considerable amount of time if you let it, but we can show you steps that will make saving money a fun and fast

part of your life. When you are organized, time at the grocery store can be a lot less time con suming than when you have no idea what you need. Brenda absolutely abhors shopping and going to the store with a plan is a welcome change for her. Now she gets in and out stress free.

Since Sara's stockpile has grown to such a sus-tainable size, she rarely even goes to the grocery store unless there is something specific she needs. When she finds a deal, like something free, or something at a rock bottom price, she stocks up on it in a fast, in and out trip to the store. There is no need to browse and spend hours if you know exactly what you need and you have your trip planned out. There are so many websites, FaceBook pages, and blogs out there on the web that even finding the deals is getting easier and easier. You can actually print them off now and head straight to store.

How much time could you shave off of your visits to the grocery store if you went in with a plan?

In a very short amount of time, you can be saving as much as you would earn with a part-time job working 15-20 hours a week. If you really don't know where to find a couple of minutes each day to work on coupons, check out this article:

http://frugalfamily.hubpages.com/hub/How-to-Find-More-Time

There are also a great number of coupon clipping services out there. These are great to use when you are just starting out too. If there is a coupon out there from two months ago, someone has it for sale! Here are a few sites to get you started:

Couponcarier.com
PowerCouponer.com

"I'm too old"

If you are not too old to shop, then you are not too old to save! By using a simple system and keeping your eyes open, you too can find the extra dollars every time you shop! The time you save in the stores, may make your life a bit easier too. If you are old enough to be on a fixed income, then you NEED to use coupons!

"What you save in coupons, you spend in gas."

Disorganization can cost you lots! This can be in the form of gas, missing coupons, or over looked deals. By staying organized and choosing your deal locations wisely, you will save far more than the cost of an entire tank of gas. Brenda saved $35 at one store on her second shop.

When you pay attention to the ads and price match what you need to buy, you only go into one store, not six or seven or eight. Sara has found a way to price match absolutely everything and therefore only makes one stop.

By price matching, marking it with a post-it note, and staying organized, you can get all the deals in one location and not have to run all over town. The only time Sara makes a second stop is when a store may be out of something os she is shopping for a specific store brand item. No one likes to run around all day at five or six different stores to get a deal.

Making things easier on yourself is the key to being successful. When couponing, you can also focus on only the stores in your area. There is no need to drive all over the state just to get a bargain because that defeats the purpose.   If Walgreens is close to you, then focus on Walgreens. If you don't want to go through the hassle of register rewards, then don't; price match at Walmart.

"I never see coupons for the things I buy "
Brenda held on tight to this one, but after her first shop, she found out how wrong she was. It's true that going extreme means get over your brand specific shopping habits- and fast but

when you can get a different brand soap or shampoo for just a few cents or even free, isn't it worth it to try something new? When you have four kids like each of us do, being brand-specific is not always an option. Our kids use any toilet paper and any kind of shampoo available because it is what we "buy".

One of the great things about living in this awesome technological age, is we have access to so many websites and vendors 24 hours a day 7 days a week. Contact your favorite brands whenever you want and request coupons for the items you prefer.

When a new product comes out companies spend big marketing dollars promoting their newest products. The newer the product, the bigger the coupon! The objective is to get you to try their product because they want you to become a loyal buyer. So trying new things is part of extreme couponing.

Sara copied a co-workers shopping list and you can see it below. The items that are circled are all items that routinely have coupons. If you could stop paying for those items, how much less money would you be spending at the grocery store?

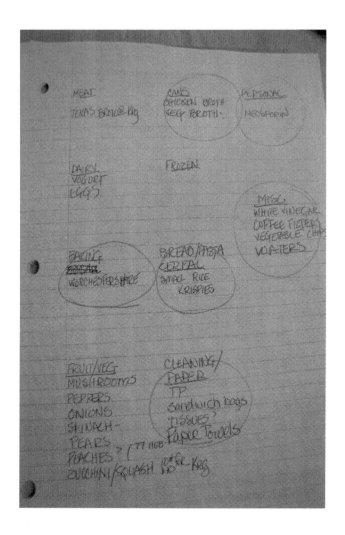

"Since that TV Show Came Out, Stores Don't Have any Deals"

It is true that many stores have changed their coupon policies since the publicity of the Extreme Coupon show. If you look at the policies however, it still allows for many sensational deals. Coupon doubling and tripling are harder to find, but there are still a few stores where this exists. Stacking sales, manufacturer coupons, and store coupons still allows for many freebies and money makers (We'll explain what these are later, but they equal great savings!).

As long as you stay aware of the store's coupon policy, then you can still find deals, and still be able to save your family major money. It is more or less a waiting game. All you have to do is have the right coupon at the right time. When the items you want go on sale, you have the coupon for it, and buy it at the rock bottom lowest price. The stores are always competing with each other. So they will always have that one item that both are putting on sale, hoping you will come to their store to buy it. That's when you as a couponer go in there and rack up on the savings. You have to find the deals. They are out there.

"I hate shopping! I just want to get in and out of the store!"
Brenda doesn't like the crowds, the lighting, the hunting, or the standing. What she found is that by being organized and prepared before she ever enters a store, she spends far less time inside! This is a great bonus for people like Brenda, but if you love to shop like Sara does, you can always lounge through the store and look for more great savings.

Once Sara built up her stockpile, her shopping list grew shorter and shorter. For example, once her personal hygiene products were stocked, she marked those off her list for a very long time.

She doesn't need to buy laundry detergent, body wash, razors, or toothpaste for a long long long time. Now she only goes into the store for items she has to buy like fresh fruit, veggies, and those types of things. She will only go to coupon shop about once a week, and that trip is always planned out and she knows exactly what she's getting. Her trip will also only include items that she can get for free or really rock bottom prices. No need to do more shopping than that.

Once you start saving loads of money, then you will **want** to go to the store to get another bargain. By staying organized and detailed in your research, you can minimize your time spent shopping and focus all that extra time somewhere else.

"Coupons hurt the local economy"

Huh? Coupons are a form of marketing. Retailers benefit from your use of coupons when they submit them to the manufacturer for reimbursement. A typical reimbursement to a manufacturer would be an extra 8 cents per coupon. If you add the numbers up, a retailer's submission of coupons can be quite profitable! Sara actually had a store manger tell her that the store lost money every time she used a coupon. This is simply not true.

As we mentioned above, manufacturers issue coupons because they want to lure you away from your normal routine. They are working hard to make new products, entice your taste buds, and solve your problems. They use coupons as an incentive for you to try something new. Isn't that nice of them?

The manufacturers have an advertising budget for commercials, ads, coupons etc. The money that they reimburse the stores for taking the coupons comes straight from that advertising budget. The manufacturers are happy for you to buy their products, coupons or not. They are just looking for some way to get their products into your home. They are happy when sales spike due to coupon usage. They are happy their products are in your home.

When a store doubles and triples coupons, they are using their budget to lure you into their store instead of the one down the street. Many stores didn't anticipate the excitement from television shows and are getting away from doubling and tripling.

It's like throwing money away

Brenda is constantly amazed at how much money she wasn't saving before she started clipping coupons. She doesn't buy processed foods and thought all of the coupons were for unhealthy products like chips and drink mixes. She was surprised that her brand specific deodorant, personal care items and shampoo regularly offered coupons in the Sunday paper.

Brenda followed an oblivious friend around the store while she did her grocery shopping. When they got to the register, she pulled out $6.00 in coupons and price matched a few items. Her friend saved nearly $20 without planning! If she hadn't used those coupons and price matched those items, she would have thrown that money away.

Sara is at the point where if she hasn't saved at least 75% of her purchase, then she hasn't done so well. Saving in the range of 85-95% is a regular thing for her. That equals up to a great deal of extra money she can use elsewhere. She'd much rather be using the money for her family in other ways than handing it over at the grocery store. "Every time I think about how much money I could have saved over the years and years of being a stay at home mom, I just kick myself!," says Sara "If I had started this when my kids were first born, then the amount of money would be astounding!"

But this book is about staying stress free, so when you come to the same realization of how much money you were throwing away, just know that you were in great company! From this moment on, you can be a saver!

More available for donations

Sara's neighbors quickly discovered her talent for finding deals and stockpiling free or low cost items. She was the one they turned to when a family of 10 lost everything to a house fire. She was able to supply them with soap, shampoo, laundry soap, dish soap, tooth brushes and toothpaste all at no direct cost to her. In all, her family donated over $250 groceries.

Donating items and time has always been dear to our hearts. Each of us is blessed with health and our own fortunes and it makes us happy to extend those blessings to others.

Sara sends items home with her sister and sister in law as often as she can. They both have several kids and times are tight for everyone. She supplies them with shampoo, soaps, food, etc.

Who could you help with a ton of free items? Do you know a single parent? Could your church use extra items? Would you send toiletry items to the troops? Couponing can help you do it!

3. Avoiding Discouragement

Seeing success stories on TV and reading about all of the free stuff others find can make you feel a little uneasy about your own trips. So you only saved $20 at the grocery store...hello? YOU SAVED $20! That is something to be happy about! If you found $20 lying on the street, would you be happy, or would you be upset that it wasn't a $100 bill? If you are still depressed, you are just a Debbie Downer anyway.

Deciding to become an extreme couponer can be overwhelming, even if you are super excited and raring to go. We've listed a few things that you can do to keep the extreme in the savings and out of the stress.

Everyone has to start somewhere.

This week you may only save $20, then the next week, you may step it up and save $40, then who knows, you could start saving $100 each trip. The savings is all up to you and how much you are willing to put into it. Sara only saved t $50 her first trip. Once she started working out the kinks and quit making some of the common mistakes, the savings got bigger and bigger. Don't get discouraged. We all had to start some-where.

Take one step at a time

You are super excited, you've watched people on TV, read about people like Sara and you are roaring to go. Whoa. Stop and take a breath. This is about to become a major part of your life, so let's take it one step at a time and it will be-come natural. There is no need to try to do it all at once. If you come at this in a slow and me-thodical pace, you will be more successful. Some couponers who jump off the deep end and try to save $500 on the first trip get overwhelmed and end up quitting. So take your time, read through this, and plan it out. You'll be a huge success!

Stay organized

Keeping everything in one place will keep you from missing out on those great deals. Keep your notebook with you in the store, in the car, and in the house. It's going to be an additional type of purse for you to carry with you wherever you go. If you have it labeled correctly, finding things will be a snap and save you lots of agony. Walking up to the register with your coupons in hand will al-ways be less stressful than desperately searching for the coupon you knew you had somewhere.

Organization goes beyond just your binder. You need to be organized in how you sort and cut your coupons, and in how you file your receipts Once you find the system that works for you, you will be more at ease and more confident in your purchases. When you stay organized, then you also stay in the game. When things get all out of whack and you end up scrounging around, then you will get frustrated and end up quitting.

This was a major challenge for Sara in the beginning. She is a spontaneous and free spirited person that can change her mind in a heart beat. She knew to be an extreme couponer she had to make sure that her binder was organized and up to date at every moment. She never knows when she will find the perfect deal that she needs to get right now. When her binder is organized and up to date, then it's no problem to jump in the car and go get that great deal.

When the coupons are where they are suppose to be and in the right places, then you can accomplish what you want when you want. Make things easier on yourself and keep it organized from the beginning!

Choose a simple system
Plan exactly how you are going to work this gig. From the clipping through the organizing, find-

ing the deals and them buying them, make sure everything you do is simple! You might be a little rough around the edges at first, but we are going to help you get through this like a pro the very first time!

Each time you work your system, it will get a little easier, a lot faster, and eventually it will become second nature. Assemble your coupons in an assembly line with your family, organize your coupons by the aisles in the store that you shop at most often, and circle the adds of the items you have coupons for with a sharpie.

What works best for Sara is cutting every coupon in the Sunday inserts every week. Her family has gotten so good at this that her girls can come in , sort the papers, all by themselves, before Sara even has a chance to glance at them. Sara will cut them and then her girls will put them in stacks according to food type or grocery category.

Some people skip the clipping completely. They organize coupon inserts by date and month and store them in folders with scissors. There are four basic coupon sources: P&G, Smart Source, Red Plum, and Unilever. You can also add a category for "other" like coupons you get in the mail, off items in the store, or online.

If you are good at researching deals online, then this may be a great system for you. When you find a deal, most websites will post the date of the insert the coupons are in for that deal. You can then go and cut that coupon and use it. This system requires you to be hyper organized before you get to the store and we don't recommend it when you first start out.

If you find a great deal that wasn't advertised in the paper or online, then you don't have a way to find the coupon on the fly and you may miss the deal entirely. That is the reason that Sara prefers to cut every coupon. This kind of system works great after you are well stocked and don't mind missing those un-advertised specials.

Find a shopping buddy

Don't do this alone! It is important to have a shopping buddy to call you up with a great item on clearance, go with you when you order 100 items that are on sale, or jump for joy with you when you stacked enough deals to get a boat load of free stuff. Your shopping buddy can be a friend, relative, partner or even a child. Just make sure this person is someone you get along with and have fun with.

If you absolutely cannot think of anyone to back you on this little adventure right now, don't worry! You will meet lots of new friends who like to save as much as you do. You might find them at a coupon exchange, on a local website, or they might spot you in the store with your nifty coupon notebook.

Brenda had a great experience in her second month of couponing. She was shopping at her local Walgreens where the manager had not placed the sales tags to the matching merchandise. She noticed that another extreme couponer was hunting for a sale item. Brenda asked if she found it and then brought an item to the cashier to price check it, and shared the information.

Later in the store, that same woman told Brenda about an un-advertised special and even gave her a few of her own matching coupons! This is a perfect example of how a shopping buddy can help. If you miss a deal, they may find it, it they miss a deal, then you might find it. Buddies are everywhere...now that you are in the club!

Sara and her shopping buddy often play "Marco Polo" around the store. They laugh and joke, but most importantly, they find deals. A shopping buddy also keeps you going. If you are getting tired or just feeling burned out, then they can pep you up and keep you clipping. Having support when couponing is key. You will always need to have someone supporting you and pushing you to do better each time. It also just makes it more fun to have someone to talk to in the store!

Use kid power

When you make couponing a family activity, you're creating a fun hobby for all of you and spending time together is a good thing! Having more than one set of eyes can help you save more. Let your kids help sort the coupons and stuff them into your notebook. Sara does this on a regular basis. She puts her kids to work sorting and organizing all the time. As a former teacher, Brenda can tell you this is a great visual discrimination exercise suitable for even a very young child.

Sara was blessed with girls who like to organize. They even get excited when organizing the stockpile. It gives them a sense of ownership in the process too.   Sorting coupons, filing them into coupon binders, and shelving all the items are all ways your family can help. We don't recommend letting kids cut any coupons. Coupons are like cash and if a mistake is made when they are cut, you don't want to blame your child!

Couponing is a great fiscal lesson. When our kids are on their own one day, they will have all the knowledge and tools they need to start their own couponing and stockpiling. They know what is involved and they know exactly what to do. At the age of 12, Sara's oldest child let her know that she "gets" the sorting, cutting and filing, but the math throws her for a loop. Her youngest "gets "the math.

Brenda scored 3 bottles of free shampoo, but only because her daughter knew they had a coupon! Don't underestimate kid power, it is very valuable.

Find a place to brag about your finds

To stay motivated, it is very important that you have a place to celebrate. Relatives are probably not the best bet for this. They might be polite, but unless they are couponing too, it can be frustrating to communicate your excitement.

You also have to be careful who you brag to because then they will expect things for free from your stockpile. Sara has experienced this from several people. They hear about all your savings then they think they are entitled to raid her closets.

Use a site like EpicCouponing.com to share your successes, and maybe a few frustrations. You'll find others who share your passion to save and they will help you keep going.

4. Recommended Supplies

The one item you should never be without

Keep a calculator with you. Retailers are getting sneaky. The biggest sizes of some items are not always the best value. Even people who do not use coupons can find a calculator very helpful. Your time is valuable and you don't want to spend it calculating the best price on a can of soup.

A 3 ring binder

A 5" D slant binder is best. Sara uses two of these. Brenda used one 2" binder and grew out of it in her second month. Use whatever you have lying around, you will grow into a new one soon enough. Sara uses two big binders. One binder holds all of her food item and the other holds everything else (the non-edible items).

Your binder should have a pocket on each side to hold your policies, store ads, envelopes and stamps.

A word of caution: Carrying around a card box or envelope is a dangerous idea. There are far too many stories about people who have accidentally left these boxes at the register. Brenda witnessed this very act. The cashier tried to chase after the owner, but was unsuccessful.

As we mentioned in an earlier chapter, when you carry the card boxes or bins, all your coupons it makes it very hard to find the right coupon at the right time. When you invest in a binder and use the baseball card holders, then you can literally see what the coupon is, the expiration date, and what the discount is just at a glance. You won't be shuffling through and getting frustrated if you start a binder from the beginning.

Sara knows this from first hand experience. She started with a card box marked with all the right categories, but quickly got aggravated at the searching and losing of the coupons. If something takes too long and ends up making you spend more time in the store, then you're not going to want to do it very often. It's too stressful.

Whatever you choose to carry your coupons with, make sure you include your first name and contact information so in the event you lose it, your hard work and savings can be returned to you!

Vinyl Holders

This makes storing your coupons and displaying them simple and your coupons will be easy to find. You can find them where ever baseball cards are found and at online stores like Amazon.

Labels

There are lots of different types out there; we like to use the sticky labels. It makes it easy to create new categories, and to move things around if you need. If you have other labels or pocket dividers lying around, make use of them!

Coupons

We are stating the obvious here: more about where to find them later.

Store Coupon Policies

Store clerks attitudes towards coupons and extreme users vary. Sometimes a clerk might not know the store policies when it comes to the use of coupons. Having a copy of a store's policy and understanding it yourself may help you out when there is confusion.

Some stores don't like to give them out. With the rage of excitement about coupons right now, many stores are changing their policies almost as often as they change the sales ads. You can usually find a store's coupon policy online at the store's website.

Store ads

Keeping these ads handy can save you a lot of time and money when you want to price match. We'll talk about price matching later. Be sure to circle the expiration date on each ad so you know when to switch them out.

Envelope

It might be tempting to just hold your coupons in your hand before you get to the till, but you need both of them to look for other coupons and check the product to make sure it matches. Doing a simple thing like bringing an envelope with you will help you protect your savings. Another simple way to keep your coupons safe is to hole punch a Ziploc bag and place it in the front of your binder.

Be very diligent about putting the coupons you are currently using in a special place so you don't have any rushing or confusion at the register.

There is nothing quite as rattling as holding up

the whole line while you search franticly for the coupon you misplaced. Other shoppers will get frustrated and you will get embarrassed.

This is another reason to have a shopping buddy, it eases the nerves. Make it a habit that whenever you put an item in your cart, you also put that corresponding coupon in the Ziploc or envelope. Don't tell yourself that you will get it later.

#10 Envelopes and Stamps

Many of today's deals come in the form of rebates. Unless it is an instant rebate, you will need to mail something to get your money. Knowing exactly where your envelopes and stamps are will make sure you don't forget to claim your cash! More on rebates later.

Car Coupon Holder:

This is where you can make use of the cute little coupon envelopes that never seemed to save you money. You've seen these coupon holders before. You may have even tried them once or twice before. They are cute, but don't really work for extreme couponing.You can make use of them by keeping one in your car. Many coupons are for things like restaurants and oil changes. Keep those handy in your car envelope.

Sharpie marker:

As you sort through various ads you will want to make notes of the coupons you have and the final cost. Using a sharpie will help you find the deals faster and with less stress to your eyes than using a regular pen.

Push a little: Paper Cutter

This will allow you to cut more than one paper at a time. It will save you a ton of time and keep you from accidentally cutting off important things like the expiration dates and bar-codes. These can cost a little bit, so if you want to wait until you see the fruits of your couponing, you have our permission to hold off for a week or two.

Here is all of our recommended supplies on one Amazon page: http://astore.amazon.com/extremecouponingwit houtextremestess-20

5. Where to Find Coupons

In your Junk Mail

Coupons are mailed to you all the time. Just take a second to look at the junk mail you receive before you toss it in the recycling bin. Owning a store credit card will often reward you with members-only coupon mailers too.

In Food Packages

Coupons are often stuffed inside food packages. Cereal, lunch meat, and pasta are all types of food that may offer some savings for your next purchase. Now that you have a coupon binder, you will keep them nice and organized and they won't clutter that junk drawer.

Buy Newspapers

Start with at least two and build up. Sara gets 20 papers and she is often asked how she gets 100 items of something at a time.

When you buy two, you can go ahead and buy that product that is on sale even if you are not sure yet if it is the best deal. It's kind of a buy one now, save one for a better deal kind of thing. Having two coupons also allows you to put odd shaped coupons in your binder back to back so that the value of the product is on one side of the plastic and the expiration date is on the other.

When you buy your papers it is important to make sure all of the coupons are in the paper. Sometimes there may have been a mistake when they were stuffed. Other times, greed has taken over and someone took more than their share of the coupons when they bought a paper.

You can have your papers delivered, but be warned that this may be more trouble than it is worth. If you use stores with register rewards, you may want to use the rewards to buy your paper and you can't do that if they are delivered to your home. You also may not buy a large amount of papers every week.

On certain holidays like Mother's Day, there are no coupons in the paper. You will pay for papers without coupons if you have them delivered.

If you have a good delivery service and your coupons are always inside your paper, then it is a real convenience to have them delivered to your house. Check with your local paper to find out how many you can have delivered at one time.

If you chose to get your coupons out of the paper, then there are a few coupon preview websites that will email you a preview of what is coming out in the paper that week. The one Sara uses most is sundaycouponpreview.com

Use Peelies

These are the little coupons that come on packages you find at the store. Now that you will have an envelope to store your coupons at the store, you'll remember to use them right away.

Push a little: Print from online

Here are some great locations to find coupons online. Typically, you can print two coupons per computer from these sites. If you can print from home and work, you are already ahead. Save yourself some money by printing on the backside of paper you no longer need.

> Coupons.com
> SmartSource.com
> RedPlum.com

Find your favorite products on Facebook. You can often find coupons for new products when you click the "like" button on the Facebook page of your favorite products.

Push a little: From your neighbors and co/workers

Soon you will be finding yourself with free things like catfood, candy bars and toothbrushes. When you get something extra, give one of the freebies to a neighbor who gets the paper delivered. They will start to see the value of your couponing efforts and will start to bring you coupons. This is also a great way to meet the neighbors that just moved in.

Bottom line is that when people see how excited you get over this stuff, they will think of you when they have a peelie, get a sample in the mail, and of course get the local paper.

Push a little: Write letters to your favorite companies or call their 800 number.

Brenda once called to let a company to let them know just how fantastic she thought the new flavor of cinnamon rolls were. She was thrilled to get coupons in the mail for some free rolls.

Another time she called the manufacturer of a new product she was using simply to ask a question. She was glad to give them her address when they asked if they could send her some coupons! She was even more delighted when the coupons were for absolutely free products.

Push a little: Get them when you order free samples

Be on the look out for free samples. They are everywhere you go and they are usually packed with coupons for the regular sized item.

Push a little: Get them from local businesses,and hotels.

Many restaurants and hotels get the paper delivered on a regular basis for their customers to enjoy. Offer to recycle the papers in exchange for keeping the coupons. You may be doing the earth a great favor. The worse that could happen is they would say "no."

Push a little: Magazines

You can get free samples of magazines when you look online. You might want to subscribe because you get them sooner than at the stores. A few of our favorites are *All You* and *Better Homes and Gardens*. Look for deals, remember to never pay retail.

Other places to find them are at professional offices. Offer to recycle them. Sara asked a doctor's office if she could have the coupons in their magazines and they actually passed her scissors to cut them all out.

It never hurts to ask!

Go Extreme: Get them from a recycling bin

As far as we are admitting, neither Sarah nor Brenda has gone to this extreme but others have had success with this and it is worth mentioning. First, realize that recycling bins are often a source of income for non-profits. Be sure to replace any paper you remove from a recycling bin so that income is not lost.

Next, be sure to bring a step stool to get into the bin and a partner to pass the stool back so you can get out. Before you enter a bin, look on the outside of the container for any instructions about who to contact to make sure you are not stealing.

Finally, bring a flashlight and know what you are looking for. Even in broad daylight, those bins can be dark and you will need the flashlight. If you don't know what you are looking for, you will waste a lot of time sifting through meaningless papers.

Frankly, it is best to get your coupons from someone BEFORE they put them into the recycling bin.

Go Extreme: Buy them from Ebay or a clipping service

Sometimes you can get starter packs that are pre-cut for a very reasonable price. It is really worthwhile if you buy things like pet food and diapers. Be careful to look for sellers with positive reviews and whose listings promise the coupons are from the paper and not internet coupons because internet coupons are often regional and will not work in different zip codes.

Do not steal

Stealing is wrong and it doesn't make sense. Unfortunately the coupon craze sometimes takes a hold of people's common sense. What one person does reflects on all of us extreme coupon people. Be respectful of the law and of others who come after you.

Using coupons other than as listed is a form of theft. Don't try to use that coupon for a sample size if it expressly says that it is only valid on the family size. There are plenty of bargains to be found using coupons the correct way so there is no need to spend time trying to pull one over on the stores.

Here are some sites to help you find coupons:

freecouponalerts.com
coupon.com
organicfoodcoupons.com

6. Assemble Your Binder

Your binder (or binders if you are going extreme) is/are the most important part of your organizational system. After you place your vinyl holders inside, you will want to place your #10 envelopes, stamps, and store policies in the back pocket. The front pocket will hold your current store ads. You are almost ready to clip your coupons. Label the inside with your name and contact information (just in case you leave it behind in all the excitement.)

Labeling

A labeling system that you understand is very important. We like to use the Avery stick on labels but any kind of label that you can read easily will work just fine. Make sure you place your labels out far enough to be seen easily when the pages are closed.

Use our list below as a guide to make the labels for your binder. You are the one who will decide where a particular item belongs. If you think it is a frozen food item, then put it under the frozen food label. If you think it is a snack item, then put it under snacks. Please don't send us a letter and ask us how to categorize a coupon. It doesn't matter how we do it; what matters is where you will look for it. Follow your own instincts and you can find the coupon when it matters.

Opening and clipping with a paper cutter

Using a paper cutter can save you oodles of time, especially if you are purchasing a large volume of coupons. The first couple of times you clip, you don't want any distractions. You will want to have a clear and quiet place to clip your coupons. Open up each section of the coupons. Stack identical pages on top of each other and make sure they are lined up on your paper cutter.

Coupon cutters and paper cutters.

Brenda asked Sara this question at her class: "What is the difference between a coupon cutter and a paper cutter?"The difference is that your coupon cutter is a money maker! You will want to take care of it and not cut anything but coupons with it. Keep it in a special money making place.

Manufacturer's Coupon and Store Coupon

It is important to understand the difference between these two types of coupons because it will affect your ability to stack your coupons. We'll explain stacking later.

A manufacturer's coupon is distributed by the company which manufactures the product. They will reimburse the store the value of the coupon and a little extra for the inconvenience of waiting for their money. A manufacturer's coupon can be used in any store where the product is sold as long as the store is willing to send them in for reimbursement (accepts coupons).

A store coupon is distributed by the store where you buy the product. These coupons are only accepted at the store who distributes the coupon. For example you could not use a Target coupon at Kroger.

Sometimes stores will put their name on a coupon and list it as a manufacturer's coupon. This is a way for them to advertise that they sell the item. In most cases, if the coupon states "manufacturer's coupon," then it is usable at any store even if it has a different store name on the coupon.

Folding coupons

Your coupons come in many sizes. When placing them inside your binder, you will want to take care to fold them in a way that makes it easy to see what the coupon is for, the value, and the amount it is worth. Smaller coupons will fit directly into the pocket but many will need to be folded in a creative way. Many times a good fold will require you to fold the middle of the coupon in and then fold the ends. Sometimes they will be so large that you will have to fold it with the product showing on one side and the expiration date on the other.

Don't go back to back

It might be tempting to place more than one type of product in each pocket, displaying them on opposite sides. This is a bad idea because as you remove coupons from the pocket, you may lose some. It also eliminates the ability to display larger coupons with a product on one side with the expiration date on the other.

Read the fine print

Many coupons show a big number on the face like $1.00 off . Then when you read the rest of the coupon it says "when you buy 2" Make sure you understand what your coupons mean so that you won't be surprised at the register.

Here are labels we recommend:

Eyes,	First Aid	Medicine
Teeth / mouth	Hair products	Body wash / soap
Deodorant	Lotion	Face products
Makeup / nails	Female items	Shaving
Garbage / Ziplocs	Paper products	Glade / Air-wick
Cleaning	Laundry	Dish soaps
Dog food	Cat food	Yogurt
Biscuits	Dairy	Frozen food
Frozen des-serts	Meat	Bread
Breakfast	Oils / baking	Spices
Condiments	Peanut butter / jelly	Rice
Meal kits		Etc (everything else)

7. Where to Find the Deals

Start with the sales ads. Many of them will show you the items that they have on sale and tell you about a matching coupon. No work! But they don't tell you everything, so we will explain more about what to look for.

Most of your sales ads will come in the Sunday papers, but you may have to wait until Thursday. Another place to get the sales fliers is from the stores themselves. Remember to find out if any of your local stores double or triple coupons.

Next, using your fliers, match up your coupons with the sales. Don't worry if you don't see many match-ups your first time. The trick is to watch closely each and every week. Use your sharpie to mark how much the items will cost you with the coupons you have.

If your favorite store matches prices, then you have it made. Use the sales ads to get the sales price at your favorite store.

Make sure you list out exactly what items you want to have price matched and circle them on your ads. Most stores require you to show the sales ads in order to match the price.

Push it: Use an app on your smart phone

The availability of phone apps changes as often as the weather in Chicago. As of the writing of this book these apps were available for no or low cost. Look for them in your phone's app store:

- Sale Price
- Swift Tally
- Coupon Sherpa
- Shop Star
- The Coupons ap
- Iq
- cellfire

Stacking

We mentioned stacking when we defined the difference between a manufacturer's coupon and a store coupon. Stacking is when you use both of these coupons on the same product.

A Target coupon is considered a store coupon, therefore you can "stack" a manufacturers coupon on top of it. For example: John Frieda shampoo and conditioner retails for $5.97, there is a Target printable coupon online for $3.00 off, and there is a $2.00 off coupon in the paper. That makes $5.00 off, making the shampoo only $.97. This can be done at any store that offers "in-store" coupons. Check you store's coupon policy before attempting this just be to sure. The majority of stores will honor this system. Stacking is a fantastic way to maximize your savings.

BOGO or B1G1

Buy one get one free. Depending on the store policy, you can often use a coupon to buy the first item and then use your B1G1 coupon to get a second item for free. When you look at these deals it can make your total cost for two items very small. For example, if you buy a deodorant item on sale for 99 cents and use a B1G1 free coupon, then the cost is less than 50 cents each when you buy two.

The magic really happens when you have a coupon. Let's say you have a coupon for 50 cents off that deodorant item. Now you can buy the first item for 49 cents and get the second item for free. The total cost of each item ends up being less than 25 cents!

Understanding Register Rewards (RR)

Rather than placing an item on sale where a competitor will match it, some stores will offer you money off of your next purchase. These incentives can often score you some free items. Here's an example: Lotion is sold for $3.99 and they will give you $3 in RR. That makes the item essentially 99 cents. If you have a $1 off coupon for that lotion, it just made you a penny!

Sara has had great luck getting her favorite store to price match the cost of 99 cents so she doesn't have to mess with the RR. Brenda hasn't had that kind of luck, so she uses the RR to buy her newspapers the next week.

When using your RR, you can make several purchases in one trip. This way they can use the RR to purchase a different item on the same day. The cashier's are familiar with this and it really isn't a big deal.

Avoid this mistake:

RR are not valid on the same item. In the example above, you cannot use the $3 in RR to buy the same lotion. You can, but you will not get another $3 in RR. Remember to use your RR to purchase different items.

CVS calls their register rewards bonus bucks and they limit the amount you can save by keeping track with your savings card. Target offers similar savings by offering you a gift card with select purchases.

Walgreens just started tracking sales with a program similar to CVS.

Out of Stock Merchandise (rain checks)

When you were counting on using a coupon at the store with a sale and they are out, ask them for a rain check. Push it a little by looking for missing merchandise on the shelf for items you were not planning on buying. This gives you another 90 days to find a matching coupon. Go extreme and purposely revisit stores at the end of the sales week so you can request a rain check.

Price Matching

Price matching is your friend! It will save you both time and gas. Find out which of your favorite stores offers price matching by asking them. If your store price matches, you can get the same low prices a competitor advertises. This is why you bring the store fliers in the pocket of your binder. Many price matching stores can adjust the price of your items right at the register so you don't need to go to the customer service area to get the best deal.

Price matching usually only applies to advertised prices and does not include register rewards or bonus bucks. If you are lucky, your store will include these extra savings.

Be careful about assumptions here. Some stores managers will limit who they match. For example one area Walmart stopped price matching Toys R Us because they said they were too far away to be competitive.

Rebates

This is an area where Sarah stays clear. Brenda has had lots of luck getting full refunds for products she buys at Walgreens.

It doesn't help much in the realm of instant gratification because the checks take a month or more to get in the mail. Brenda always enjoys opening checks!

To make rebates worth while, make sure to keep the rebate form and your receipt in your binder. When you get your item home, vow to send it off right away! Manufacturers count on you forgetting to send in the required information. They really do lose money every time someone sends in a rebate.

Money Makers

These are super fun. When you find a sale, and stack a coupon on top of it, sometimes you will come out ahead. For example, when Sara found cat treats on sale for 50 cents each, she used $1.00 coupons to buy 30 of them. She made $15 dollars that trip which she used to buy other items (and yes she owns a cat.)

Watch your store policies when it comes to money makers. Some stores, like Target, have a policy against it. As of the writing of this book, Target will reduce the amount of the coupon to match the purchase price of the item. You can still get your items for free with this policy but you won't get a money maker. Sometimes, you are able to add additional items and the money comes off of that price. Brenda was able to get fee bananas in addition to the free dishwasher detergent at Target this way.

Pushing it:

Buy items that you won't use if they are money makers. Even if you don't own a cat, you could use those $1.00 coupons mentioned above and donate the food to your local animal shelter. Better yet, bring them to the lady down the street struggling to get by on Social Security. The idea is to buy the product, make the money and make sure the item gets used, even if it's not by you.

Extreme:

Only buy certain items when they are free. This is like holding off on buying that spaghetti sauce because you know it is going on sale soon. Holding out for the free items gets easier as you build your stockpile. We'll tell you more about that later.

Catalina:

This is not an Italian restaurant. A Catalina is a coupon that prints out with your receipt. You get money off of the item you just purchased during your next visit. When you visit the deal sites we listed for you, you know where to go to get these goodies to print out.

Brenda was super excited her 2nd week when she was able to get 5 Wonka Bars for the price of one using Catalinas. She purchased the first one and passed the Catalina to her daughter. When her daughter bought hers for $0, it still printed out a Catalina and she passed it to the next kid. All of the kids were super happy to get free chocolate that day!

Understanding Sales Cycles:

Ever notice your favorite brand of spaghetti sauce goes on sale every month or so? You intuitively stock up a little and when you start to run out, you know that it should be going on sale again soon. Maybe there are certain items that you only buy when it goes on sale.

Here is a big secret and a huge "aha!" Coupons usually do not match sales right away. This is why so many people think that coupons are "not worth it." You need to watch those sales and store coupons and hold onto your coupons until that super deal arrives. Being aware of the sales cycle of your products will help you realize when it is time to cash them in. It is a little like stocks only much more profitable!

When you get a handle on the sales cycles, you'll know what you need to build your stockpiles. Some items like toilet paper only go on sale every three months, and other items, like make-up are on sale every week. When you pay attention to the cycles of the items you buy, it will be easier to know how much you need before the next sale.

Great Websites to help you find deals:

Many of the sites below will do the coupon matching for you. That means, all you need to do is have an organized system of coupons. They will tell you which sales items having matching coupons.

www.epiccouponing.com
www.coupondivas.com
http://thekrazycouponlady.com
http://wildforwags.com/
http://www.totallytarget.com/
http://wildforcvs.com

8. Getting Though the Checkout

Profile the cashier

Look for a cashier who is having a good day. If you are asking to ring up items separately, stacking coupons and price matching, it certainly helps to have a cashier who is cooperative. Usually young men are the easiest to work with. Pay attention to who's line you go through and get to know your cashier. Even if things don't go as expected, realize that they are just doing their job. Make a friend and you have another partner in saving.

Have coupons in hand

You are already taking longer than the average person when you go through the check-out line. Make sure that you are ready by having your coupons in your hand when you go into the check out lane.

This is made easier if you pull them out when you put the related items into your cart. This is a great time to check and make sure that your item is an exact match to your coupon. Place them in a temporary envelope and you will be prepared when you get to the till.

Watch the register

When a cashier spots you as a couponer, they are actually pretty careful to make sure that each of your coupons go through. Be aware. Sometimes sales items don't ring up accurately, and other times valid coupons don't go through. Be sure and keep your cool if something doesn't work properly. It is a mistake, but it could be your mistake!

Brenda found that Walgreens usually takes about 15 minutes to update their registers on Sunday mornings so many of the sales do not ring up properly first thing in the morning.

We can't stress enough here, that you must keep your cool. Brenda had a manager try to keep her coupons valued at $8 each for some make up. She said there was a fax that came in saying they should not accept them because of the high value. Brenda had to ask 3 times for the woman to return the coupon. Then she took them to another store and used them without the hassle. If she had lost her cool, Brenda may not have had her coupons returned in usable order.

Bring a friend/kid/partner

Avoid mistakes by bringing a loyal helper. The spouse who is constantly nagging at you "are you done yet" is not the one to bring with you. You need someone who will help you count your items three times making sure you bought the right amount to get your $10 in savings. Your partner should be able to flip through your coupons as you shop for the things on your list. They can save you time by getting the coupons, reading the fine print, and they might spot an extra savings!

Kroger often has sales that give you $10 savings when you purchase 10 of a specific list of items. Brenda was heart broken when she missed her savings by one item. If she had brought one of her daughters that day, she wouldn't have missed out on the savings!

The friendly cosmetics counter lady

When you shop at a smaller store like CVS or Walgreens, you might find it more convenient to bring your items to the cosmetics counter. This avoids long lines at the regular check out and you can breathe easier. After a trip or two, your cosmetics counter lady or gentleman will recognize you and may have a tip or two to share. They often admire the savings you get and will tell you about deals other people have been getting earlier in the day.

What to do when you meet resistance

Sara was thrilled to get her order of 100 soda bottles that were on sale at her local grocery store. She got to the register and handed over the 100 coupons she had ready in hand. She was met with less than enthusiasm. Without getting into detail, Sara was escorted out of the store without her soda.

Having a partner with you for support is important. You don't know what people's frame of reference is when they meet you with hostility. Maybe they had a bad experience with another crazy coupon lady. What ever it is remember to keep your cool. Kill them with kindness. Smile, and always be polite.

Show them the store's coupon policy. Politely ask to see the manager. If necessary, ask for the store number and the contact information for the corporate office. Be careful and consider carefully if it is worth while to make waves. If this is the store you like to shop at most often most often, it may be wise to let things go.

9. What is a stockpile & Do I need One?

Only you can decide

Sara has taught the secrets of couponing to masses and the biggest dilemma among them is often the same; they can't build a stock pile. Stockpiling is not for everyone, but if you want to cut your time hunting deals and browsing the grocery store, then stockpiling is a must.

The idea is to find free or insanely cheap items and buy a ton of them. Done right, you won't have to purchase more until it goes on sale again. Buying only a few papers will get you only a few items. Sara buys twenty papers at a time and this allows her to buy 20 items at a time.

Here's an example, she bought 20 sale item detergents for $1.49 each, spending $29.80 for all of them. That's less than the $15 she used to spend on 2 bottles of "cheap brand" detergents. Having 4 kids, she regularly spent $30 a month on detergent. Twenty bottles of detergent lasts her a very long time and she can mark it off of her shopping list for months.

When an item is free, you can buy even more. Sometimes Sara has over 50 tubes of toothpaste in her closet and she knows she won't run out before she can find them again for free. Sometimes organizing a stock pile is cumbersome, but it can also be lots of fun to see all the items you've collected without spending your hard earned money. One thing in your stockpile is one less thing on your list!

How to find storage space

The biggest thing to remember is that you want to be able to find your items after you have found a place to store them. If you store similar items in the same place, it will be much easier to find them than if you tuck them away in a different spot every time you find a deal. For example, store all of your shampoo, regardless of the name brand in the same bag, box or storage bin.

Be careful about putting things in a shed or a garage. You don't want your brand new items to freeze or be exposed to extreme heat. Food items should always be inside your home so they don't attract rodents or other unwanted pests.

If possible, store items in the room where you will use them. For example, use the linen closet or bathroom closet for things like shampoo and toothpaste. Use the pantry for items like dish soap and pasta. You get the idea.

Use the space under your bed with drawers, the space above your cabinets with clear boxes, and the drawers of the empty china cabinet.

When things get too tight, it means your stock-pile is growing! Now you can look for even more creative ways to store your items.

Creative ways to add more space

Storing your items might be very easy if you are starting off slow, but you might be surprised how quickly your stockpiles will grow! Here are some creative ways to add more space:

Plastic Bags on Hangers

In a pinch, store items in the bag they came in. Loop the bag directly over a hanger and store it in your closet. Use a long piece of masking tape to label the hangers so you can find your items quickly.

Over the Door Shoe Storage

These are great for storing all of those sample size items that are hard to find. Instead of stuffing them into a drawer, put them in the see through plastic for an easy find.

Push a little: Garage Lift Storage System

Again, you want to be careful not to expose your finds to extreme temperatures, but if your garage is temperature controlled, it might be a great place to store your stockpile. Some people use stand up shelving, but if you need that room for your cars, you might consider one of these. They cost just over $100 but compared to the amount of money you are saving by having a stockpile, it is money well spent. Remember to never pay retail!

Go extreme:

Use a spare bedroom or other room in your house exclusively for your stockpile. Sara built walls in an unused dining room and used it exclusively for her deals.

Not recommended:

Do not store items in places that have extreme weather conditions like a hot garage or damp basement. Your items will be ruined and your efforts for naught.

Do not store your items in places out of your reach. That cabinet above your refrigerator is not the best place to store the toothpaste.

Do not store items where they will attract bugs or vermin. Accidents happen, and spilt food is a sounding horn to bugs. Storing food items on the floor is never a good idea unless they are in an air tight container.

You can find a shoe storage system and garage lift on the Amazon page we created at :

atore.amazon.com/extremecouponingwithoutext remestess-20

10. Let's Get Started!

Your first day

Buy your papers. Look for a store that discounts Sunday papers. Remember to check and see if all of the coupon fliers are in them.

Cut out everything, even if it is for dog food and you don't have any pets. Believe it or not, this will save you time. You will not have to do any mental calculations, you just cut. When you start pushing and going extreme, you will be finding money makers even in your unused categories. These are also great to have for coupon exchanges.

Sort them into your categories. You can use the categories we listed for you or make your own. Next stuff them into the vinyl inserts of your notebook.

Now look through your sales ads while the coupons you cut are still fresh in your head. You have cut and stuffed, and now you are bound to find at least one good deal. Is it a free or outrageously cheap item? Go get it!

Now that you have your first super deal, write it down, jump for joy, go on line and brag!

Your first week

Build your momentum by keeping all of your receipts and logging how much your new habit saved you in just one week. Ravage through your favorite store's sales ad. With your freshly cut coupons nearby, find out which sales match your coupons. Circle the item in the ad with your sharpie and write down how much the item will cost you with the coupons. If you are feeling really ambitious, go ahead and check out the sales ads of other stores.

Spend some time getting familiar with deal sites such as totallytarget.com and wildforwags.com These sites will let you know what coupons matches are available and how to match them with the upcoming sales. Read the forums on epiccouponing.com and you can find unannounced specials and deals that others post as they find them.

Week 2 and beyond:

Add one paper
Now that you've seen how much you can save, its time to buy another newspaper,or another 18! As your confidence and your savings grow, you can add more papers to the mix.

Add one method
Once you have the coupon and sales matching down, you can look for other ways to save. It is time to see about price matching, online coupons, and potential rebates. Now that you've

gotten started, keep going. It won't take much effort because you will soon be addicted!

Check your coupons

About twice a month you will want to give your notebook a thorough check. Seeing the expiration date of your coupons will help you decide if you know if you are running out of time to you use a favorite coupon. It will also keep the coupons you have top of mind so when you see an un-advertised special in the store it will pop out at you.

When you find coupons that are expired, remove them right away to make room for new ones. This will keep you from being disappointed at the store when your expired coupons don't work.

What to do with expired coupons

Military bases over seas have more time to use coupons. You can adopt your own base at ocpnet.org and send them directly or you can find a local organization who will ship your coupons for you. Separate your items into food and non-food items (this is easy if you use two binders like Sara.) Send your coupons in baggies without rubber- bands or paperclips and send them as quickly as you can.

Join coupon exchanges

As you get more comfortable using your coupons, you'll find other like-minded individuals. If there are no coupon exchanges near you, you can start your own!

Exchange bins at stores

Don't overlook these little gold mines at the store. You can often find a basket of coupons at the customer service area. When you find a coupon you can use, make sure you swap it out with one you won't!

What to do with left-over papers

Buying 20 or more newspapers bring up an important problem. Many people choose to recycle the papers but here are a few more creative ways to use the papers:

- Use it as wrapping paper,
- Start a compost,
- Stuff your sneakers to take the smell out
- Start a worm farm.
- Make paper mache'
- Donate them to school art teachers

11. Keep the Extreme in Your Couponing

It's about what is best for you and your family

Sara and Brenda both have 4 kids. They don't coupon the same way. Neither is stressed about it. Find your way by trying it out.

Enjoy the new products and the great savings. Start your stockpile and build it up. Pay attention to the savings and don't stress about the near misses.

Stay grounded and keep your cool. When you are approachable, you will make many new friends and have a great time while saving money! Don't forget to post your brag stories at EpicCouponing.com!

.

Made in the USA
Middletown, DE
06 December 2014